PRAYING
with JESUS

D1279400

PRAYING
with JESUS

DVD STUDY GUIDE

Six Sessions for Groups and Individuals

JAMES BANKS

Discovery House.
from Our Daily Bread Ministries

© 2016 by Discovery House

All rights reserved.

Discovery House is affiliated with Our Daily Bread Ministries,
Grand Rapids, Michigan.

Requests for permission to quote from this book should be directed to:
Permissions Department, Discovery House, P.O. Box 3566, Grand Rapids, MI 49501.
Or contact us by e-mail at permissionsdept@dhp.org.

All Scripture quotations, unless otherwise indicated, are taken from the HOLY BIBLE,
NEW INTERNATIONAL VERSION.® NIV.® Copyright © 1973, 1978, 1984, 2011
by Biblica, Inc.™ Used by permission of Zondervan. All rights reserved worldwide.
www.zondervan.com

Bible verses quoted in the appendix are from the *Holy Bible*, New Living Translation,
copyright © 1996, 2004, 2007 by Tyndale House Foundation. Used by permission
of Tyndale House Publishers, Inc. All rights reserved.

Study guide questions written by Dave Branon

Interior design by Sherri L. Hoffman

ISBN: 978-1-62707-535-0

Printed in the United States of America
First printing in 2016

CONTENTS

INTRODUCTION

Imagine what it would be like to pray with Jesus. Think of all you could learn from Him, just listening as He spent time with His Father. Imagine hearing Him praying for you and interceding for others. What you would learn would encourage you to pray for the rest of your life!

There's no better teacher on prayer than Jesus. His guidance on prayer—not only what He said about it, but also how He did it—brought a fresh and vital understanding to what it means to have a relationship with God.

Jesus's approach to praying is practical and powerful. In *Praying with Jesus*, we'll review some overlooked and unexpected ways He talked with His heavenly Father, ways that will help us keep company with God as well. We'll take a deeper look at what it means to call God "Abba, Father." We'll examine the priority Jesus placed on prayer and the difference this makes for everyday life. We'll learn from the ways Jesus used Scripture when He prayed. We'll also consider what Jesus taught about faith and persistence in prayer when it seems like nothing is happening. And we'll see Jesus's example of loving others with His prayers—examining a special promise He made to believers who pray together.

If you've ever struggled with praying, you'll find inspiration here. Jesus is an example like none other! Come, join us on the adventure as we discover the help only He can give.

SESSION 1

ABBA, FATHER

 # THE WAY

Where We're Headed in This Session

Have you ever wondered: *How important* is *prayer, really*? That thought could trouble our minds if we have the wrong focus—especially if we use prayer as a pragmatic way to "get what we want." But as James Banks explains in Session 1 of our study, there is so much more to prayer than that. James points out some astounding facts about Jesus and prayer that will give us a sense of awe about this marvelous privilege. And he reminds us that the essence of prayer is not results but relationship. How important is prayer? As our heart-to-heart connection with the one true God, it's absolutely essential!

Starting Off
Talk about prayer:

1. With the group, share your doubts and concerns about prayer. What about prayer challenges you?

2. Discuss some instances when prayer gave you comfort and courage in your life—regardless of the answers you received.

Along the Way

As you watch the video, pay special attention to the following:

- how many times Jesus prayed or taught about prayer

- why Jesus is praying even today

- what "Abba, Father" indicates

- an amazing fact about prayer from the book of Revelation

- what Augustine said about our spiritual need

THE TRUTH

Perspectives from Life and God's Word

Video 1: Abba, Father

(Use the space provided to take notes on James's lesson.)

MAIN IDEAS

Our experience and the disciples' question for Jesus

Jesus, the prayer example and teacher

Jesus is _____ praying for us right now!

Abba means _____

God as Father

James's dad and the mug

"This beautiful privilege"

The "breathtaking picture" of Revelation 5:8

God's reaction to our prayers

When we pray, we declare our _____ on God

Augustine and "restless hearts"

THE LIFE

Applying the Truths We've Learned

1. As you think about James's teaching for this session, what stands out to you most?

2. The video session began by listing a number of troubling issues people have with prayer: finding time to pray, getting distracted, not knowing what to say, lack of answers. Discuss how these or other issues affect your view of prayer. Which of these have you faced, and what other problems have arisen? How do you respond to these issues?

3. In this session, James mentions that Jesus made twenty references to prayer in His teaching, and that He prayed on at least thirty-one different occasions. Refer to the Supplemental Information listing on page 20, which details those instances. Choose one or more of each as time permits, read them aloud, and discuss.

4. James said this about Jesus: "He is still praying for us right now!" Look up and read the following verses, which tell us this amazing truth: 1 Timothy 2:5; Hebrews 7:25; 1 John 2:1. Then discuss what this truth means to you as you live this sometimes difficult life on earth.

5. There are three references in Scripture to the concept of "Abba, Father." In Mark 14:36, Jesus uses the phrase during an extremely troubling moment. In Romans 8:15 and Galatians 4:6, the apostle Paul suggests that *we* can use the name. Compare these references, and discuss the comfort they can give believers.

6. What story might you have like James's story of his dad's mug—a treasured experience of love shared?

7. James calls Revelation 5:8 a "breathtaking picture." What do you think of this idea that God preserves your prayers? What does this mean to your prayer life?

8. As James discusses Galatians 4:6 and the idea of "Abba, Father," we can see that prayer is less about getting stuff from God and more about relationship with Him. Discuss this idea of prayer as a way of "keeping the lines of communication open" with our heavenly Father.

9. James says, "God does want us to bring our needs to Him—but that's only the beginning." And, he adds, "God wants to give us Himself." Discuss how can we see prayer more as a way to enhance our relationship with God—which is truly the key to a joyful life.

10. Augustine said about God, "You have made us for yourself, and our hearts are restless until they find rest in you." How can prayer help us calm our restless hearts and find peace in our heavenly Father?

Living the Life
Ideas for action:

1. Using the list mentioned in question 3, take time to examine Jesus's prayers and His teaching on prayer. Consider one prayer and one teaching each day until the list is complete.

2. Contemplate whether your prayer life needs to move from mostly asking God for things to enhancing your relationship with Abba, Father. How can you make this change?

3. Consider the fact that Jesus is preserving your prayers (Revelation 5:8). How might this help you view prayer with more seriousness?

REMEMBERING THE WORD
A key verse to memorize:

> *By [the Spirit] we cry, "Abba, Father." The Spirit himself testifies with our spirit that we are God's children.*
>
> Romans 8:15

PRACTICING PRAYER
A suggestion for this week:

Spend time thinking what it means to call God "Abba, Father." Try addressing Him by that title as you pray.

For Further Reading
Related books by James Banks:

- *Praying Together*
- *Prayers for Your Children*

Supplemental Information
Jesus's life of prayer:

Jesus's Teaching on Prayer		
Matthew 5:44	Matthew 26:41	Luke 18:9–14
Matthew 6:5–8	Mark 9:25–29	Luke 21:36
Matthew 6:9–13	Mark 11:17	John 14:13–14
Matthew 7:7–11	Mark 11:24	John 15:7
Matthew 9:37–38	Mark 11:25	John 15:16
Matthew 18:19–20	Luke 6:28	John 16:23–24
Matthew 21:21–22	Luke 11:5–13	

Examples of Jesus Praying		
Matthew 11:25–26	Mark 8:6	Luke 24:30
Matthew 14:19	Luke 3:21	Luke 24:50
Matthew 14:23	Luke 5:16	John 11:41–42
Matthew 19:13	Luke 6:12	John 12:27–28
Matthew 26:39	Luke 9:18	John 14:16
Matthew 26:42	Luke 9:29	John 17:1–26
Matthew 26:44	Luke 10:21	Romans 8:34
Matthew 27:46	Luke 11:1	Hebrews 5:7
Mark 1:35	Luke 22:17–19	Hebrews 7:25
Mark 6:41	Luke 22:32	
Mark 7:34	Luke 23:34	

SESSION 2

DECLARING DEPENDENCE

 # THE WAY

Where We're Headed in This Session

We value our independence, wouldn't you say? We want to make our own decisions, drive our own car, have our own space. But being independent isn't always best for us. Making our way through this complicated and demanding world often requires us to work together as a group—or to have significant others in our lives to offer guidance, help, and assistance. Our most significant "Other" is God, and we must approach our relationship with Him in humble dependence. As James Banks points out in Session 2, "we all need God's help just to get through the moment." As you work your way through this lesson, you'll be encouraged by this vital reminder about the importance of God-dependence in prayer.

Starting Off
Talk about depending on God:

1. Discuss a time you realized you had to be dependent on God, or perhaps share when you *should* have depended on Him but decided to go your own way.

2. Who is your favorite Bible character who depended on God for help—and got it?

Along the Way

As you watch the video, pay special attention to the following:

- what James's mom said about depending on God

- what Jesus said was the "one thing" needed

- what Jesus taught the disciples about prayer

- how James and Cari prayed during their crisis

- how Hezekiah used prayer in a time of danger

THE TRUTH

Perspectives from Life and God's Word

Video 2: Declaring Dependence

(Use the space provided to take notes on James's lesson.)

MAIN IDEAS

James's mother: "Just trust God"

Turning worries into _____

Mary and Martha's conflict

Key truth from John 5:19 and John 15:5

The prayer of a demon-possessed boy's father

The disciples' question

Prayer and the search for a missing daughter

"Because you prayed" (Isaiah 37:21)

 THE LIFE

Applying the Truths We've Learned

1. Let's start with James Banks's concluding question: "What will only happen if we pray?" Discuss some situations you face that God alone can solve. Consider: Have you been praying with total trust?

2. When James told his mom in frustration, "It's not that simple!" was he echoing feelings you've had about prayer? What was Mrs. Banks trying to teach her son?

3. Consider the fact that God helped Mrs. Banks at a time when she was not able to help herself. Discuss that story and how it relates to her continually saying, "Just trust God." Things certainly turned out well for her—how does remembering God's faithfulness in the past help us as we face the future?

4. Read Luke 10:38–42. Martha was concerned about serving refreshments; Mary was more interested in sitting at Jesus's feet. We need food, but Jesus said Mary chose "what is better." What does He mean by His statement, "Only one thing is needed"?

5. In John 15:5, Jesus says, "I am the vine; you are the branches. If you remain in me and I in you, you will bear much fruit; apart from me you can do nothing." James Banks says, "Jesus wants us to welcome His presence and power into everything we do." How are prayer and our dependence on God reflected in this Bible passage? How are they reflected in James's comment?

6. James also makes this key statement: "The point Jesus makes clear here is there are some things that will happen only when we pray." Can you think of times when you know prayer was the determining factor in your own life situations? If you can't think of such a time, what could that mean about prayer in your life?

7. In a crisis, we often favor action over quiet contemplation. Discuss James and Cari's decision to spend more time talking to God about their daughter and less time frantically searching for her. Can you think of specific Scriptures that would support their decision?

8. Read Lamentations 3:22–23. How does this encouraging passage about God's mercy relate to the concept of being dependent on God in prayer?

Living the Life
Ideas for action:

1. Create your own saying or acronym about prayer—something you can use as a reminder that you are God-dependent, and that prayer is your connection to Him. Display it where you'll be regularly reminded—your computer, your bathroom mirror, or your car's dashboard, for example.

2. List some things in life that you normally depend on—and then write next to each a way you can replace it with a dependence on the heavenly Father.

3. This week keep a journal of the mercies of God that are new every morning. You may be surprised by the breadth of the list!

REMEMBERING THE WORD
A key verse to memorize:

"I am the vine; you are the branches. If you remain in me and I in you, you will bear much fruit; apart from me you can do nothing." —Jesus in John 15:5

PRACTICING PRAYER
A suggestion for this week:

As you pray this week, begin by repeating the heartfelt cry of the demon-possessed boy's father: "I do believe, but help me overcome my unbelief." Use that as your declaration of dependence on God.

For Further Reading
Related book by James Banks:

• *Prayers for Prodigals*

SESSION 3

PRAYING THE PRAYERS OF THE BIBLE

 THE WAY

Where We're Headed in This Session

Think about the words of Jesus—the prayers of Jesus, actually—during moments of crisis in His life. For instance, consider the wilderness temptation when Satan sought to trip up Jesus, or the time our Savior hung on the cross in agony on our behalf. As James Banks explains in this third segment of *Praying with Jesus*, at key moments in His life, the Lord prayed Scripture in His conversations with God. Is this something we can do too? In this session, James suggests that when we don't know what to say in our own conversations with God, the best course of action is to follow Jesus's example—praying the words of the Bible. Read on, and watch this lesson transform your prayer life!

Starting Off
Talk about praying "the Jesus way":

1. Consider and discuss the usual makeup of your prayers. Do they usually or seldom include God's Word?

2. Have you ever had times when you wanted to pray but simply didn't know what to say? What were those situations? Why was it hard for you to pray?

3. Read Psalm 22:1–2. Discuss whether or not you knew that the first words of Psalm 22 were the same as Jesus's agonized words from the cross.

Along the Way

As you watch the video, pay special attention to the following:

- how James's funny story about his brother illustrates our occasional inability to communicate in prayer

- some examples of Jesus and His Bible-based prayers

- what kinds of prayers—including praise, confession, wrestling, help-needed, and blessing—are found in Scripture

- what we learn from the Lord's Prayer

THE TRUTH

Perspectives from Life and God's Word

Video 3: Praying the Prayers of the Bible

(Use the space provided to take notes on James's lesson.)

MAIN IDEAS

The "naked truth" about struggling with prayer

Jesus prayed—and even sang—God's Word

Jesus's prayers from the cross

God's Word is alive! (Hebrews 4:12)

Prayers of praise

Prayers of confession

Wrestling prayers

Cries for help

The Lord's Prayer, point by point:

Our Father

Your kingdom

Our daily bread

Forgive us

Temptation

The kingdom, etc.

THE LIFE

Applying the Truths We've Learned

1. In James's lighthearted story about boys being boys—and Mom being Mom—what was his point? Have you ever reached a point in life when you simply did not know what to say?

2. Discuss a time in your life when you wanted to talk to God but you just didn't know what to say. How was that crisis resolved?

3. Read Matthew 4:1–11. Using a resource like BibleGateway.com or a concordance, look up the source of Jesus's three replies to Satan's challenges. How can any of these passages help us in a time of need?

4. Was it a new idea to you that Jesus *sang* from Psalms 113–118? Discuss this concept. How might this realization change the way that you pray?

5. Read Psalm 9:1–2. Notice the number of times David says, "I will," in these two verses. Read the passage again, emphasizing those two words each time they occur and noticing the four separate actions they introduce. How determined are you when it comes to pursuing God energetically in prayer?

6. How surprised are you by the psalmist's first words of Psalm 10: "Why, LORD, do you stand afar off?" What does this tell us about God? How willing is He to listen to our struggles and even our wrong assumptions about Him?

7. James asks a great question: "Have you ever prayed the Lord's Prayer on autopilot?" How can we use the Lord's Prayer as a heartfelt cry to our Father rather than a simple recitation? (Note: James gives several examples as he breaks the prayer down into sections.)

8. James quotes 2 Timothy 3:16–17, but his use of this passage is a bit different from what we often hear. How does this passage encourage us when we are trying to pray the prayers of the Bible?

Living the Life
Ideas for action:

1. Keep track of your prayer opportunities in a notebook. Record the times you struggle in prayer, wondering what to say. Also note the times you used Scripture as a part of your prayer. See if this starts a transformation of your prayer life.

2. In the Supplemental Information on page 41, you'll see a list of examples of biblical prayers. Select three of those and write them on paper. Then pray them back to God as part of your prayer time. Try to develop a new habit of praying the prayers of the Bible.

REMEMBERING THE WORD
A key verse to memorize:

> LORD, you are the God who saves me; day and night I cry out to you. May my prayer come before you; turn your ear to my cry.   Psalm 88:1–2

PRACTICING PRAYER
A suggestion for this week:

Take James's six-part breakdown of the Lord's Prayer and pray one section each day Monday through Saturday. Let each section direct your prayer over areas of your life that you should talk about with God.

For Further Reading
Related book by James Banks:

- Praying the Prayers of the Bible

Supplemental Information
Examples of biblical prayers:

To Praise and Honor God

Exodus 15:2–3

Nehemiah 9:5–6

Psalm 9:1–2

Ephesians 3:20–21

Jude 1:24–25

To Say Thank You

Psalm 28:6–7

Psalm 30:11–12

Psalm 139:13–18

Revelation 7:10, 12

Revelation 11:15, 17

To Strengthen Faith and Give Ourselves to God

Psalm 19:7–11

Psalm 51:10–12

Psalm 73:25–28

Psalm 119:105, 111–112

John 17:1–3

Prayers about Everyday Needs

Psalm 23:1–6

Psalm 65:9–13

Psalm 84:10–12

Matthew 6:9–13

For more complete listings, consult the appendix on pages 73–77 and the Discovery House book Praying the Prayers of the Bible.

NOTES

SESSION 4

SIT, STAY, PRAY

 THE WAY

Where We're Headed in This Session

One of the most remarkable prayer answers in the Bible is found in Daniel 9. As an Israelite exiled to Babylon, Daniel offers up a prayer to God regarding the conclusion of his people's captivity. And, amazingly, *while Daniel is still praying,* God sends an answer by way of an angel, who arrives before Daniel finishes the prayer. Here's the challenge for us: sometimes we have to wait for answers to our prayers, and waiting is hardly ever easy. In Session 4, James Banks helps us deal with this reality, giving us advice on how to persevere in praying.

Starting Off
Talk about waiting:

1. Can you recall a time when you had to be extremely patient as you awaited an answer to an important prayer?

2. Discuss some biblical cases you know that required people to practice patience in prayer.

Along the Way

As you watch the video, pay special attention to the following:

- how Big Boy, the "praying" dog, resembles us

- what a persevering pastor teaches us about prayer

- what Matthew 7 and Luke 11 say about prayer

- how a Canaanite woman (in Matthew 15) provides an example in prayer

- what Jesus said and did in response to the Canaanite woman

- how waiting can lead to a breakthrough

THE TRUTH

Perspectives from Life and God's Word

Video 4: Sit, Stay, Pray

(Use the space provided to take notes on James's lesson.)

MAIN IDEAS

How we are like Big Boy when we think about prayer

Lessons from the Brooklyn Tabernacle

Sit, stay, pray: three little words with big meaning

"Keep on asking," "keep on seeking," "keep on knocking"

The dramatic story of a woman who needed Jesus' help

Jesus's initial reaction to the woman

The disciples' response to the woman

The give-and-take between Jesus and the woman

Jesus's comment: "Woman, you have great faith!"

James Banks's explanation of the story

The value of *waiting* in prayer

 # THE LIFE

Applying the Truths We've Learned

1. James Banks says, "We all wrestle with time and prayer, don't we?" Discuss some ways this happens for you. What are the biggest obstacles to making time for prayer?

2. Do you know someone who is a "prayer warrior"? What characteristics does this person display as he or she makes prayer a high priority in life?

3. What circumstances have you have faced in life that challenged your patience in prayer? Have you ever asked, "Why doesn't God answer?" or "Does He even care?"

4. Read Luke 18:1–8. What are three lessons about prayer you see in this parable of Jesus?

5. After telling the story of the Canaanite woman (Matthew 15), James discusses things we can learn from her example. Discuss what you recall about these segments of her story:

- How the woman approaches Jesus

- Who this woman requests help for

- Why "Jesus did not answer a word"

- How the woman persisted, despite Jesus's silence

- How Jesus responded, twice

- What the woman meant by saying, "Even the dogs eat the crumbs that fall from the master's table"

- How Jesus responded in the end

6. James alludes to Lamentations 3:22–23, which says that God's compassions ("mercies" NKJV) are new each day. How does that encourage persistence in prayer day after day?

7. According to James, "just being in God's presence through prayer has a way of changing us and helping us understand that somehow, He is enough." Think about prayers that don't get immediate answers or that result in God saying no. What additional benefit do we get from simply praying with perseverance, regardless of the answer?

Living the Life
Ideas for action:

1. Journal the timeline of your prayer requests. List a specific request, the times and circumstances of your prayer for that request, the answer (or the experience of waiting for the answer), and what being in God's presence in prayer has done for your faith.

2. Purchase some mustard seeds and keep them in your "prayer space," wherever you spend the most time in prayer. Use them as a reminder that Jesus said, "If you have faith as small as a mustard seed . . . nothing will be impossible."

REMEMBERING THE WORD
A key verse to memorize:

> *"Will not God bring about justice for his chosen ones, who cry out to him day and night?"*　　　　Luke 18:7

PRACTICING PRAYER
A suggestion for this week:

Think about prayer not as an effort to get God to do what you want, but as an opportunity to keep company with Him, knowing that His mercies are new each day. Practice quieting your spirit in Him as you go through the day and praising Him for His faithfulness even when answers haven't yet come.

For Further Reading
Related books by James Banks:

- *Praying Together*
- *Praying for Prodigals*

 NOTES

SESSION 5

GIVING THE GIFT OF PRAYER

 # THE WAY

Where We're Headed in This Session

Looking for the perfect gift? In Session 5 of this study of Jesus and prayer, you'll hear that "Jesus shows us that one of the best ways to love someone is to pray." As James Banks explains, Jesus demonstrated His concern for others throughout the New Testament—by praying for the sick, for specific disciples, for children, and even for us. And James shares two amazing stories of parental prayers that help us see the intrinsic and practical value of praying for others—it's a gift that allows us to access the authority of heaven on behalf of the people we care about.

Starting Off
Talk about praying for others:

1. Can you think of a time when the only thing you could give someone was your prayer? What was that like? If you don't have a personal story, share what you know about the prayers of others making an amazing difference in someone's life.

2. What is the longest time you have prayed about a specific situation? Has it been resolved, or are you still bringing it before God?

Along the Way

As you watch the video, pay special attention to the following:

- how Jesus is interceding for us

- how often Jesus prayed for others

- how James and Cari prayed for their son

- what Jesus's nickname "Friend of Sinners" means

- how Augustine's mother, Monica, prayed for her son

- the difference between power and authority in the spiritual realm

THE TRUTH

Perspectives from Life and God's Word

Video 5: Giving the Gift of Prayer

(Use the space provided to take notes on James's lesson.)

MAIN IDEAS

Jesus is _____ for us (Romans 8:34)

Examples of Jesus praying for others

James and Cari's prayers for their son, and the prayers of others

James's realization that those prayers had been answered affirmatively

The value of the testimony of answered prayer

Jesus's mission (Luke 19:10)

J. Sidlow Baxter's quote about prayer for loved ones

Monica's amazing prayers for her son Augustine

James and his son's discussion on Jesus's authority

 # THE LIFE

Applying the Truths We've Learned

1. One of this session's most intriguing ideas is that Jesus is interceding for us (Romans 8:34). Imagine that for a moment. How does that apply specifically to you right now?

2. James mentioned several examples of Jesus praying for others: for His disciples (Luke 6:12–13); as He healed the deaf man (Mark 7:34); for Peter (Luke 22:31–32); for children (as told in Matthew, Mark, and Luke); for all believers, in His own day and in the years to follow (John 17); for His enemies while He hung on the cross (Luke 23:34). Which of these is most poignant to you?

3. Readers of his book wrote to James to tell him things like this regarding his wayward son: "As we pray for our kids, we're praying for yours too." Discuss times when you have been buoyed by the assurance that others were talking to God about your needs.

4. Do you have a story like the Banks' experience with their son, prayer, and a positive outcome? As his son said, "It's pointless if others don't hear about it." Would you be willing to share your story with others?

5. James suggests that praying in Jesus's name means that we pray for what He came to earth for: that others will know God and have a relationship with Him. How can we begin to incorporate those kinds of prayers for people we know or just know about?

6. According to James Banks, "God wastes nothing. God is even able to take the most difficult things in our lives and bring good from them." As you think about tragedies, trials, and tribulations you have endured, how has this been true in your life?

7. Who are some people who need your gift of prayer? What actions might you take to help you to remember to pray for them regularly?

Living the Life
Ideas for action:

1. Using the list you compiled in question 7 above, make a point to spend time praying for each person. Then send a note or an e-mail or a private Facebook message letting these people know that you are interceding on their behalf.

2. In Matthew 11:19 and Luke 7:34, Jesus was derisively called "a friend of . . . sinners." In Luke 15:2, He was accused of welcoming sinners and eating with them. Write down three important things you learn about Jesus in these verses—and think about how those things can be incorporated in your own life.

REMEMBERING THE WORD
A key verse to memorize:

> When [Jesus] led [the disciples] out to the vicinity of Bethany, he lifted up his hands and blessed them.   Luke 24:50

PRACTICING PRAYER
A suggestion for this week:

If you have a friend or relative who does not know Jesus as Savior—someone Jesus came "to seek and to save"—spend dedicated time asking God to break into that person's life through the Holy Spirit. Then ask for God's help to keep praying as long as it takes to see a positive result.

For Further Reading
Related books by James Banks:

- *Prayers for Your Children*
- *Prayers for Prodigals*

SESSION 6

PRAYING WITH JESUS

 # THE WAY

Where We're Headed in This Session

We never really pray alone, because the Holy Spirit "helps us" when we pray (see Romans 8:26–27). But God's Word also encourages us to pray with others. In this study, James Banks gives us examples from contemporary life and from Scripture of the importance of believers praying together. The earliest believers "joined together constantly in prayer" (Acts 1:14) and found God meeting them in unexpected ways. This is a vital truth as we seek to live with Jesus today.

Starting Off
Talk about praying together:

1. Tell about a time when you prayed with someone and found your prayers to be particularly helpful.

2. Clearly, the people you worship with have differing personalities. Do you consider yourself outgoing or more introverted? How do you think you will respond to this session?

Along the Way

As you watch the video, pay special attention to the following:

- what God did with a "hog-fat prayer"
- how an elementary school band can represent our prayers
- what Matthew 18:19–20 teaches about prayer
- what God's "manifest presence" is
- how prayer helped Jan through breast cancer treatments
- how early Christians prayed together (Acts 1:14)
- what role prayer plays in "Great Awakenings"

THE TRUTH

Perspectives from Life and God's Word

Video 6: Praying with Jesus

(Use the space provided to take notes on James's lesson.)

MAIN IDEAS

Kevin's need for prayer and the church's "less than perfect" efforts

The positive result and Kevin's response

"If two of you on earth *agree* . . . " (Matthew 18:19)

The implications of the word *agree*

The power of gathering in Jesus's name (Matthew 18:19–20)

The prayer for Jan, and her response: "Whatever happens, all will be well"

The first Christian church and how the believers prayed

Praying for a "Great Awakening," and the example of Billy Graham

E. M. Bounds's quote on what prayer "moves"

 THE LIFE

Applying the Truths We've Learned

1. Consider the opening story. Ephesians 3:20 tells us that God "is able to do immeasurably more than we ask or imagine." Have you ever experienced an answer to prayer that was beyond your expectations?

2. How should we respond when our heartfelt prayer doesn't result in an answer like Kevin received? What do we learn about prayer (and God) when the sick person doesn't recover or the job we prayed for does not materialize?

3. What comfort do the words of Matthew 18:19–20 offer: "For where two or three come together in my name, there am I with them"? How does Jesus's special promise of His presence speak to you personally?

4. In light of Acts 1:14 ("They all joined together constantly in prayer"), consider the following statement by James Banks: "God designed praying together to bring life to His church." What priority do *you* place on the opportunity to pray with others?

5. James broaches an important subject relating to today's society, noting that our world could use a new "Great Awakening"—a time when masses of people turn to Jesus. How can we encourage our own congregations to pray for a fresh moving of God's Spirit in our churches, nation, and world?

6. In concluding this session, James says, "Sometimes we get discouraged with prayer, especially if we think of it only in terms of requests and answers. But Jesus shows us that there's more to it than that. It's about a relationship with someone who loves us more than life." How can we rethink our attitude toward prayer, seeing it as a way of simply keeping company with Him?

Living the Life
Ideas for action:

1. Many of the suggestions in the book are directed at individual believers. However, this session suggests the benefits of joining with others in prayer. Look for opportunities to do that in the days to come.

2. The next time someone requests prayer from you, volunteer to quietly pray for him or her in that moment. You will automatically have the "two" of Matthew 18:19–20!

REMEMBERING THE WORD
A key verse to memorize:

> [The apostles] all joined together constantly in prayer, along with the women and Mary the mother of Jesus, and with his brothers. **Acts 1:14**

PRACTICING PRAYER
A suggestion for this week:

Does someone in your church have a major prayer need? Encourage your church leaders to follow the James 5:14 pattern, loving that person by meeting with him or her to pray.

For Further Reading
Related book by James Banks:

- *Praying Together*

 # NOTES

APPENDIX

Scripture's Prayers (Selected)

Prayers to Praise and Honor God

"The LORD lives! Praise to my Rock! May God, the Rock of my salvation, be exalted!" 2 Samuel 22:47

I will praise you, LORD, with all my heart; I will tell of all the marvelous things you have done. I will be filled with joy because of you. I will sing praises to your name, O Most High. Psalm 9:1–2

As for me, I will sing about your power. Each morning I will sing with joy about your unfailing love. For you have been my refuge, a place of safety when I am in distress. O my Strength, to you I sing praises, for you, O God, are my refuge, the God who shows me unfailing love. Psalm 59:16–17

"You are worthy, O LORD our God, to receive glory and honor and power. For you created all things, and they exist because you created what you pleased." Revelation 4:11

Prayers to Say Thank You

You have turned my mourning into joyful dancing. You have taken away my clothes of mourning and clothed me with joy, that I might sing praises to you and not be silent. O LORD my God, I will give you thanks forever! Psalm 30:11–12

It is good to give thanks to the LORD, to sing praises to the Most High. It is good to proclaim your unfailing love in the morning, your faithfulness in the evening. . . . You thrill me, LORD, with all you have done for me! I sing for joy because of what you have done. O LORD, what great works you do! And how deep are your thoughts.   Psalm 92:1–2, 4–5

I give you thanks, O LORD, with all my heart; I will sing your praises before the gods. . . . I praise your name for your unfailing love and faithfulness; for your promises are backed by all the honor of your name. As soon as I pray, you answer me; you encourage me by giving me strength.   Psalm 138:1–3

Prayers to Strengthen Faith and Give Ourselves to God

"O Sovereign LORD, you have only begun to show your greatness and the strength of your hand to me, your servant. Is there any god in heaven or on earth who can perform such great and mighty deeds as you do?"   Deuteronomy 3:24

Create in me a clean heart, O God. Renew a loyal spirit within me. Do not banish me from your presence, and don't take your Holy Spirit from me. Restore to me the joy of your salvation, and make me willing to obey you.   Psalm 51:10–12

"Glorify your Son so he can give glory back to you. For you have given him authority over everyone. He gives eternal life to each one you have given him. And this is the way to have eternal life—to know you, the only true God, and Jesus Christ, the one you sent to earth."   John 17:1–3

Prayers about Everyday Needs

Many people say, "Who will show us better times?" Let your face smile on us, LORD. You have given me greater joy than those who have abundant harvests of grain and new wine. In peace I will lie down and sleep, for you alone, O LORD, will keep me safe.   Psalm 4:6–8

My heart has heard you say, "Come and talk with me." And my heart responds, "LORD, I am coming."   Psalm 27:8

As for me, since I am poor and needy, let the Lord keep me in his thoughts. You are my helper and my savior. O my God, do not delay.
Psalm 40:17

Prayers to Confess Sin and Humble Ourselves

How can I know all the sins lurking in my heart? Cleanse me from these hidden faults. Keep your servant from deliberate sins! Don't let them control me. Then I will be free of guilt and innocent of great sin. May the words of my mouth and the meditation of my heart be pleasing to you, O LORD, my rock and my redeemer.   Psalm 19:12–14

LORD, don't hold back your tender mercies from me. Let your unfailing love and faithfulness always protect me. For troubles surround me—too many to count! My sins pile up so high I can't see my way out. They outnumber the hairs on my head. I have lost all courage. Please, LORD, rescue me! Come quickly, LORD, and help me.   Psalm 40:11–13

"O God, be merciful to me, for I am a sinner."   Luke 18:13

Prayers for Guidance and Direction

O LORD, I give my life to you. . . . No one who trusts in you will ever be disgraced, but disgrace comes to those who try to deceive others. Show me the right path, O LORD; point out the road for me to follow. Lead me by your truth and teach me, for you are the God who saves me. All day long I put my hope in you.   Psalm 25:1, 3–5

You, O Lord, are a God of compassion and mercy, slow to get angry and filled with unfailing love and faithfulness. Look down and have mercy on me. Give your strength to your servant; save me, the son of your servant. Send me a sign of your favor.   Psalm 86:15–17

"What should I do, Lord?"   Acts 22:10

Prayers for Help and Protection

"O Lord, God of Israel, you are enthroned between the mighty cherubim! You alone are God of all the kingdoms of the earth. You alone created the heavens and the earth. Bend down, O Lord, and listen! Open your eyes, O Lord, and see!"   2 Kings 19:15–16

Bend down, O Lord, and hear my prayer; answer me, for I need your help. Protect me, for I am devoted to you. Save me, for I serve you and trust you. You are my God. Be merciful to me, O Lord, for I am calling on you constantly. Give me happiness, O Lord, for I give myself to you. O Lord, you are so good, so ready to forgive, so full of unfailing love for all who ask for your help. Listen closely to my prayer, O Lord; hear my urgent cry. I will call to you whenever I'm in trouble, and you will answer me.
                                                                    Psalm 86:1–7

O Lord, God of my salvation, I cry out to you by day. I come to you at night. Now hear my prayer; listen to my cry. For my life is full of troubles.
                                                                    Psalm 88:1–3

O Lord, protect your people with your shepherd's staff; lead your flock, your special possession.   Micah 7:14

Wrestling Prayers

O Lord, why do you stand so far away? Why do you hide when I am in trouble?   Psalm 10:1

Why am I discouraged? Why is my heart so sad? I will put my hope in God! I will praise him again—my Savior and my God! Now I am deeply discouraged, but I will remember you. . . . I hear the tumult of the raging seas as your waves and surging tides sweep over me. But each day the LORD pours his unfailing love upon me, and through each night I sing his songs, praying to God who gives me life.   Psalm 42:5–8

LORD, you always give me justice when I bring a case before you. So let me bring you this complaint: Why are the wicked so prosperous? Why are evil people so happy? You have planted them, and they have taken root and prospered. Your name is on their lips, but you are far from their hearts. But as for me, LORD, you know my heart. You see me and test my thoughts.   Jeremiah 12:1–3

"I do believe, but help me overcome my unbelief!"   Mark 9:24

Blessing Prayers

"Blessing and honor and glory and power belong to the one sitting on the throne and to the Lamb forever and ever."   Revelation 5:13

"May the LORD bless you and protect you. May the LORD smile on you and be gracious to you. May the LORD show you his favor and give you his peace."   Numbers 6:24–26

Now may the Lord of peace himself give you his peace at all times and in every situation. The Lord be with you.   2 Thessalonians 3:16

 NOTES

ABOUT THE AUTHOR

James Banks, founding pastor of Peace Church in Durham, North Carolina, has a doctor of ministry degree from Gordon-Conwell Theological Seminary and a master of divinity degree from Princeton Theological Seminary. Dr. Banks and his wife, Cari, have two adult children. He is the author of several Discovery House books, including *Praying Together*, *Prayers for Prodigals*, *Prayers for Your Children*, and *Praying the Prayers of the Bible*. Visit his websites at jamesbanks.org and prayersforprodigals.org.

Note to the Reader

The publisher invites you to share your response to the message of this book by writing Discovery House, P.O. Box 3566, Grand Rapids, MI 49501, USA. For information about other Discovery House books, music, or DVDs, contact us at the same address or call 800-653-8333. Find us on the Internet at dhp.org or send e-mail to books@dhp.org.